BOB DYLAN
Alias Anything You Please

BOB DYLAN

Alias Anything You Please

TY SILKMAN

TITAN BOOKS

For Geoff and Rosemary, who first turned me on to this stuff.
What language is he singing in?

The author would like to express his gratitude for the help received
from the following people during the preparation of this book:
Jeff Bench, Chris Bentley, Dave Dingle, Marcus Hearn, Glen Marks,
David Pratt, Richard Reynolds, Ray Tedman, Ian Woodward,
and all at Rex Features.

Bob Dylan
ISBN: 9780857685568

Published by
Titan Books
A division of Titan Publishing Group Ltd.
144 Southwark St.
London
SE1 0UP

This edition: October 2011
9 8 7 6 5 4 3 2 1

First published in the UK 2008.

Designed by Chris Bentley.

A CIP catalogue record for this title is available from the British
Library.

Printed and bound in China.

Did you enjoy this book? We love to hear from our readers.
Please e-mail us at: **readerfeedback@titanemail.com**
or write to Reader Feedback at the above address.

To receive advance information, news, competitions,
and exclusive offers online, please sign up for the Titan
newsletter on our website: **www.titanbooks.com**

CONTENTS

'There will be time, there will be time
To prepare a face to meet the faces that you meet'

T S Eliot, 'The Love Song of J. Alfred Prufrock',
from *The Complete Poems and Plays of TS Eliot*, Faber, 1965

'I didn't create Bob Dylan. Bob Dylan has always been here...
always was, when I was a child there was Bob Dylan.
And before I was born, there was Bob Dylan.'

'Why did you have to play that role?'

'I'm not sure. Maybe I was best equipped to do it.'

Interview with Jonathan Cott, *Rolling Stone*, 16 November 1978,
reprinted in *Dylan on Dylan*, Hodder, 2006, p.269

The 1981 European tour

PREFACE

Bob Dylan: Alias Anything You Please is a book of photographs. It's not a biography, and it is emphatically not a critique of Dylan's songs, lyrics and music. However, the text and captions of this book do attempt to perform a kind of critique of Dylan as the subject of the photographer's camera. Dylan the icon, Dylan the performer, even Dylan the clothes horse.

Such an endeavour might seem to be a very trivial pursuit – at least to some – when compared to the task facing the critic who sets out to interpret Dylan's lyrics, music, or prose writings – the critic who attempts to explain Dylan the creative artist, in all of his provocative contradiction and complexity. And – let's get this out of the way up front – Dylan himself has fired off many scathing attacks on those foolish or naive enough to over-interpret his work, to see meaning where no such meaning was intended. So why bother?

Dylan was (and remains) a public figure created and sustained by the mass media. He is, of course, much more than a mere 'celebrity' – to use a word devalued to the point of meaninglessness by a culture that places footballers' wives, has-been politicians, surgically-modified models and waspish royal butlers on an equal and [ob]noxious plateau. But Dylan's art, delivered as it has always been through the machinery of the mass media, is not immune to the inflections of that machine and has – most remarkably of all – left indelible marks on the workings of the media machine itself. Dylan's stellar trajectory through the sixties and beyond actually changed, in some degree, the nature of stardom, fame and celebrity. And this was chiefly because Dylan became the first

celebrity not to play the media game by its established rules.

That's what makes all those press conference assaults on uncool journalists – such as the memorable encounter with *Time* reporter Horace Judson in *Don't Look Back* – so momentous, and so funny. Dylan's personal critique of society was implicit in all of his public statements. Refusing to play along with the dumb questions of journalists, throwing their banal and presumptuous platitudes back in their faces, was itself an act of rebellion in an era when pop stars were still expected to fit meekly into a safe, predictable mould. Four decades later, of course, the abrasive language of 'attitude' has become as banal as the old-school showbiz clichés it was intended to overturn. But that's another story...

Which brings us back to the photographs themselves. Over and over, the camera captures something in Dylan that corresponds to the mood, the image, the attitude of his songs – whether it's the introverted folk singer, the leather-jacketed rocker, or the suede-jacketed country crooner. To put it simply, the camera likes him. And the camera always captures Bob Dylan: it almost never sees Robert Zimmerman, whoever he may be. Perhaps only Clark Kent, with his x-ray vision, could pull off that journalistic assignment. But as Dylan himself has been so energetic throughout his career in moulding and adapting his image to ensure that it never contradicts his art, perhaps we should not regard it as a futile endeavour to explore Dylan's photographs as a way to understanding – a little more deeply – Dylan the artist and Dylan the performer.

The colossal blue and purple shirt

One
FAME AND FORTUNE

'It was impossible for me to observe anything now without being observed.'

Bob Dylan, *Chronicles: Volume One*, p.121

Bob Dylan is an assumed identity, as has been pointed out on many occasions. When the 19-year-old Robert Zimmerman decided to create him, he had previously created at least one performing alter-ego. That alter-ego had been Elston Gunn, rock and roll sideman. Gunn was another Boy from the North Country, a rock 'n' roll piano player who auditioned for Bobby Vee's backing band and was disappointed not to get a permanent gig. There have been other aliases – Blind Boy Grunt, Bob Landy – but only one that really matters.

Much has been written (anecdote, theory, analysis) about the aptness of Zimmerman's choice of Bob Dylan. Without going too far into that discussion, it's clear enough that the name Bob conveys some of the timeless, classless, regionless essence of the Everyman. The wandering Everyman of American myth and popular culture, all the way from Walt Whitman and John Dos Passos to Woody Guthrie and Jack Kerouac. And the name Dylan (whatever story you believe about the reasons behind its choice), has the double resonance of the poet Dylan Thomas and the perhaps equally significant Marshall Dillon of Dodge City. A singer who is everyman, a poet who is also a gunslinger bringing his own brand of justice to a lawless frontier town. Perfect. Sufficiently complex to point in several directions at once. Sufficiently accessible, yet sufficiently exotic, for any fan to identify with the implied unstarlike star persona.

'A poem is a naked person. ...some people say that I am a poet.'

[Bob Dylan, *Bringing It All Back Home*]

So, by inference, a singer could be someone who has to go about in clothing. Something, at any rate, to cover the nakedness of poetry. As it happens, the covers of five Dylan albums in sequence – from *Blonde on Blonde* to *New Morning* – depict the singer wearing a suede jacket of some kind. The music and the songs on each of these albums are very different. Does this mean something? After all, the Big Bubba of Rebellion, the Czar of Dissent, the Buddha in European Dress, has to wear something to hide his nakedness. The Emperor – at least in public – has to wear clothes. But the critics are always hungry for signs. Roland Barthes once wrote, apropos of the Abbé Pierre, that the idea of fashion is antipathetic to the idea of sainthood. Reflecting on the late sixties, on the time when he became absorbed in being a family man, Dylan writes 'My outer image would have to be something a bit more confusing, a bit more humdrum.' The suede jacket, in the late sixties, certainly fitted the bill. The rock star burned out by touring gets to chill out and get his head back together in the country.

Jann Wenner: 'What is your day-to-day life like?'
Bob Dylan: 'Hmmm – there is no way I could explain that to you, Jann.'

[Interview with *Rolling Stone*, 29 November 1969, reprinted in *Dylan on Dylan*, p.151]

Can Bob Dylan really have a day-to-day life? Perhaps that kind of thing is only for the Robert Zimmermans of the world. From 1967 to 1971, Dylan grew a beard. It was never a particularly luxuriant growth, but it did achieve a certain condition appropriate to beardedness. Dylan wore his hair long, but not especially long by the prevailing standards of the time, i.e. the standards generally applied to rock singers. Dylan had always worn his clothes the way regular people wear their clothes – because he liked them. For evidence of this, watch the footage with Bobby Neuwirth in the Newcastle clothing store from *Don't Look Back*. No image consultant is pulling the strings in that scene.

Take just one example. In photographs of Dylan taken in 1965, we encounter a particular blue and purple shirt. It turns up over and over again. You'll see it in this book – sometimes photographed in full colour, sometimes in black and white. If anyone has a desire to found a new branch of Dylan scholastic crankery (or quackery?), researching the true history of that shirt would be a good place to start. It's clearly what Dustin Hoffman in *Midnight Cowboy* calls 'a colossal shirt'. It's a shirt that announces in no uncertain terms that Dylan's days as a folk singer are over. From now on the wearer is going to be performing electric music. Rock. And he'll be dressed for the part.

Dylan is wearing the colossal blue and purple shirt on the front cover of *Highway 61 Revisited*. He's wearing it in the photographs with Joan Baez taken on the Victoria Embankment in London in May 1965. On the *Highway 61 Revisited* cover Dylan is also wearing a Triumph motorcycle t-shirt. He liked motorbikes. Crank critics have concocted theories to explain what the t-shirt has to say about the meaning of the album's lyrics. No one has – as far as I know – had much to say about the colossal shirt. But the message of both – as well as the whole outfit, and the pose, and the pale nite-owl complexion – are all proclaiming the same thing. 'Here's the new Dylan. Electric Dylan. Don't judge him by the standards of the old one.'

In *Chronicles*, Dylan quotes Tony Curtis as saying that fame is a full-time occupation. Dylan, more than any other performing artist of our times, has learned to live with his fame without submitting to the demands of the machine that sustains it. But Dylan also confesses in *Chronicles* that people expect that fame and money will translate into power, but this is not always the case. The common ground between the star and the man in the street is the media, and the blurring of reality and fantasy that the contemporary media accomplish. As Dylan remarked in 2002: 'We live in a world of fantasy, where Disney has won... Fantasy has become the real world. Whether we realise it or not....'

In *Moondust*, an account of the Apollo astronauts who walked on the moon and returned to Earth to accept fame and incomprehension in equal measure, Andrew Smith makes some telling comments on the contemporary process of media-based adulation:

'Old-fashioned fame was acquired, but celebrity is bestowed: it only exists in relationship with the audience-jury we supply and comprise.... We voted them in and we can vote them out, more immediately and effectively, in fact, than the politicians who themselves look and behave more like celebrities every day.... fame has a hinterland, but the boundaries between the two conditions [fame and celebrity] have become so confused that we no longer recognize this distinction. *So you'd better sign the autograph, sucker. You're lucky I even ask.*'

[Andrew Smith, *Moondust*, Bloomsbury, 2006, p.156]

Moondust is a *Don't Look Back* narrative for the Apollo astronauts. It maps out many of the same stages of negotiation with fame and fortune that we catch glimpses of in the camera's observation of and relationship with Bob Dylan. Some travellers in the kingdom of fame do manage a return journey now and again.

Opposite: The Embankment, London, 1965

28 April 1965, with Dana Gillespie

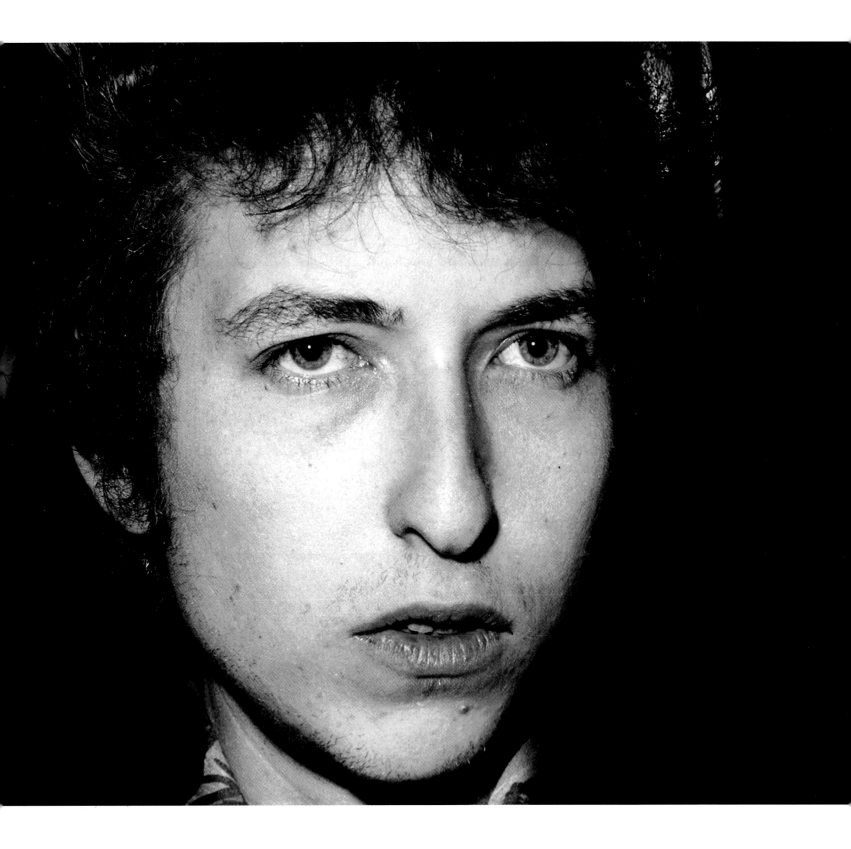

In Columbia studios, August 1965, recording 'Highway 61 Revisited'.
The 'police siren' used on the song can be seen in Dylan's mouth.

Portrait, 1965

Portrait, 1978

Late 1977, California, publicity shot

Opposite: In concert at Wembley Arena, London, 1984

The Cat in the Hat, 1984

Sydney, Australia, 1986,
at a press conference in the studio
of Australian artist Brett Whitely

Opposite top: With Jack Lang, receiving the French Academy Arts and Letters Award, 1990
Opposite below: At the Golden Globe Awards, 2001, with Phil Collins at extreme right

Fame as a form of incomprehension.
Bob Dylan's old sofa, placed at auction in November 2004.

Dylan in the role of Billy the Kid's sidekick, Alias, in Sam Peckinpah's *Pat Garrett and Billy the Kid*

Two
PERFORMING

'I wanna be entertaining as well as truthful.'

Bob Dylan, 1965

It has not (how shall we say?) always been exactly Dylan's way to ingratiate himself with his audience. Not for him, on stage, the standard greetings and intros. 'Hello London, are you ready to rock?' 'Get out of the bar, you can buy your drinks later on...' 'Now I'd like to do a song from my next album, called...' Maybe this reticence, in part, goes back as far as Dylan's earliest days as a basket house performer in New York, or back even earlier to Minneapolis. ('Basket houses' because performers passed around a basket to collect the money.) Don't give anything away. Or is it just impatience with the conventions of performing? Not wanting to do what everyone expects. Chatting up the audience, the artiste's ingratiating patter, this is all a part of the traditional showbiz dimension of rock. The patter of the magician who distracts the audience from the conjuring trick. Dylan has had nothing to do with all of that.

...Except, during his tours in the immediate aftermath of *Slow Train Coming*, the Born Again tours. On those tours, Dylan would regularly address the audience direct, spelling out the significance of particular songs, or just preaching on the state of the world and the imminence of Armageddon. But this distinction only points out the general dissonance of that period from Dylan's performing career. And, moreover, the preaching and exposition from the stage were in response to audience hostility and incomprehension of Dylan's new Born Again Christian repertoire. Most people will finally react if they are pushed long and hard enough – such as the famous moment when Dylan called out 'I don't believe you, you're a liar' to the heckler calling him 'Judas' in the Manchester Free Trade Hall on the 1966 UK tour.

Instead of engaging his audiences with semi-scripted

stage patter, Dylan's approach to performing has always been to create the appropriate persona to deliver the songs. This persona embodies every aspect of the Dylan the audience experiences, from details of the actual performance (what voice? which guitar?) to less strictly musical considerations. It's these considerations of expression, gesture, body language and appearance that the camera unblinkingly records.

Dylan hadn't always been a deadpan performer. In his early days in New York, he was renowned for his ability to keep an audience entertained in between songs. Clinton Heylin quotes Arthur Kretchmer's recollection of the 1961 Dylan in *Dylan: Behind the Shades*:

'On stage he was essentially a funny character. Maybe that isn't what he intended to be, but the audience reaction was one of laughing, not at but with Dylan...'

[*Dylan: Behind the Shades*, Clinton Heylin, Penguin, First Edition 1991, p.39]

This aspect of Dylan's stage persona was marginalised during the protest period, the electric to motorcycle crash period, and the country retreat period that followed – almost a decade. But it re-emerged in the most unlikely way – as the keynote of Dylan's performance in Sam Peckinpah's *Pat Garrett and Billy the Kid*, in which Dylan plays a secondary gang member, a quirky sidekick to Kris Kristofferson's Billy. Dylan's character is known as Alias.

GANG MEMBER: Alias what?
DYLAN: Alias anything you please.

Dylan as Alias in
Pat Garrett and Billy the Kid

Dylan and Kris Kristofferson in
Pat Garrett and Billy the Kid

Pat Garrett and Billy The Kid.
Dylan with director Sam Peckinpah.
Peckinpah takes a memorable cameo role in his own
movie, as a coffin maker. 'You know what I'm gonna
do? Put everything I own right here, I'm gonna bury it in
this ground and and I'm gonna leave the territory. When
you gonna learn you can't trust anybody, even yourself,
Garrett?' he tells James Coburn's Pat Garrett.

'...the Peckinpah experience was valuable in
terms of getting near the big action....
They don't hire people like that to make
movies any more...

Bob Dylan

Dylan's portrayal of Alias in *Pat Garrett and Billy the Kid*
is one of the most enigmatic performances of his career.
The film was scripted by novelist Rudy Wurlitzer – author of
The Octopus, a kind of late-sixties take on Kerouac's *On
the Road*, and screenwriter of cult movie *Two-Lane
Blacktop*. Wurlitzer knew Dylan and was instrumental in his
involvement. Wurlitzer's screenplay for *Pat Garrett and Billy
the Kid* is a knowing and sophisticated reworking of the
familiar cowboy legend. The central story, of newly-
appointed lawman Pat Garrett's protracted search for and
eventual cold-blooded shooting of his former accomplice

Billy the Kid, is overlaid with narrative devices and
symbolism that represent this hoary old yarn as a metaphor
for the generation gap. The film is also an elegiac vision of
the end of the Old West, as the wide-open spaces of New
Mexico are fenced off with barbed wire. Peckinpah is
concerned, as he is elsewhere, with the impossibility of
honour in a world of shifting loyalties – a circumstance that
was also reflected off-screen as the final cut of the movie
was taken out of the director's hands by MGM. Dylan,
observing all that took place, determined to assume total
control of his next movie project, *Renaldo and Clara* (1978).

Dylan the acoustic performer, 1964

As Dylan has grown older, and as he went out on the road more and more, it seems as if the opposite aspects of his performing persona have grown closer together. At one end of the spectrum comes the Chaplinesque clown from *Pat Garrett and Billy the Kid*. Perhaps we see a more edgy version of this persona in the MTV-style show-card routine that accompanies 'Subterranean Homesick Blues' at the opening of *Don't Look Back*. At the opposite end of the scale is the hellfire preacher who took to the road in 1979. This persona may have been foreshadowed by the narrator of the songs (at least some of the songs) on *John Wesley Harding*, and even the folk-protest persona seen most unambiguously on *The Times They Are A-Changin'*. The contemporary Dylan of the early twenty-first century, the Dylan of *Love and Theft* and *Modern Times*, appears to have integrated these disparate personalities into a rounded whole.

Looking for the personality behind a performer's art can be a little bit like looking through the layers of a glass onion – the image that John Lennon used to describe the press and public's clumsy perception and misunderstanding of an artist's private life and public work. Our admiration betrays us into making foolish imaginings about those whose work we admire. Lennon intended the phrase as a put down of journalistic blundering ('expert, textpert' he taunts in 'I Am the Walrus'), but the glass onion image is not a bad metaphor for the kind of performer Dylan has always been. Closer to the mark, at any rate, than 'The Buddha in European Dress' or 'The Big Cheese'. The famous Dylan/Lennon London summit in the back of a limousine in 1966? Big Cheese meets Glass Onion.

3 May 1966, Mayfair Hotel, London, press conference

The 1966 tour

15 May 1966, at the De Montfort Hall in Leicester, UK.
Walking on stage for the second (electric) half of the set.
Left to right: Dylan, Robbie Robertson, Garth Hudson
(with his back to the camera).

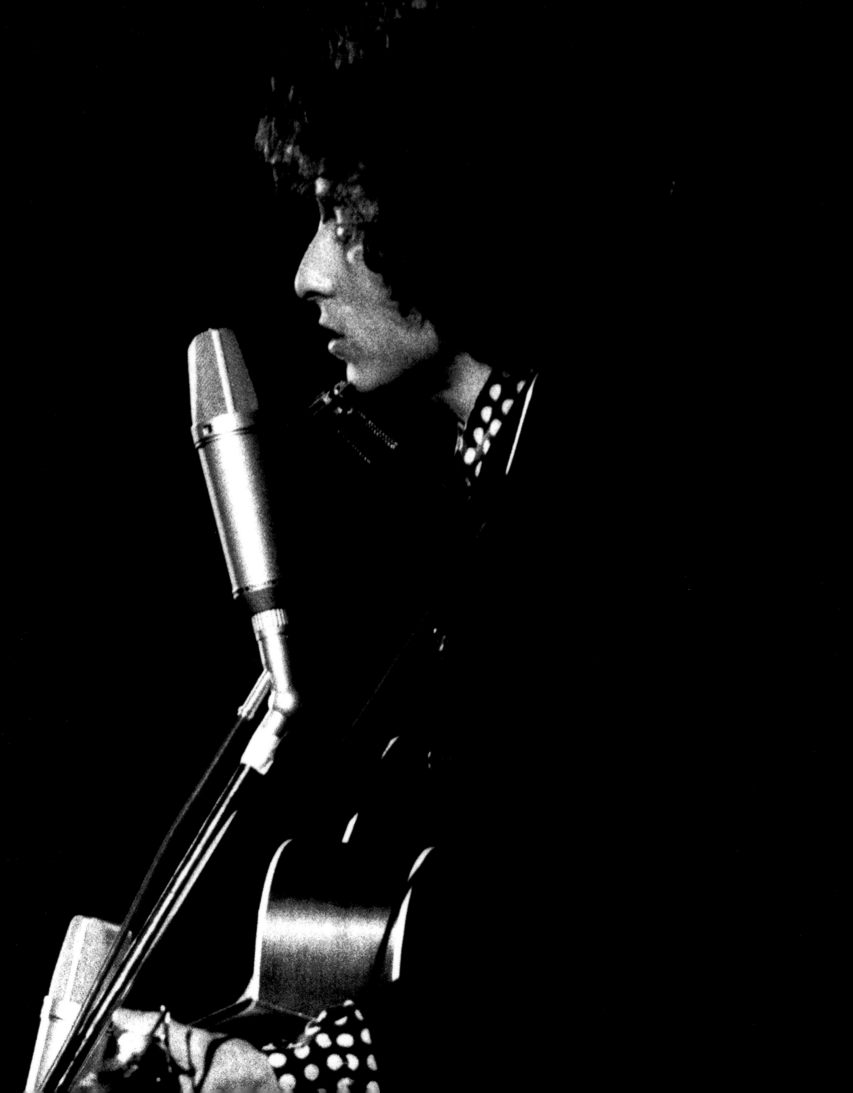

A cautious return to public performing in 1969 saw Dylan appear on the TV show *Johnny Cash – The Man His World His Music*. The backdrop designed for Dylan's comeback performance originally included a fake backwoods-style one-room country shack. Dylan wisely insisted that this prop be removed.

Opposite and following pages: 31 August 1969: The Isle of Wight Festival. Dylan was reported to be nervous before stepping onstage for this comeback performance. He had scarcely performed in public for three years. Although reunited with The Band, the set played was a mix of earlier songs such as 'She Belongs to Me' and 'Like a Rolling Stone' and material from the already-bootlegged *Basement Tapes*, such as 'Minstrel Boy and 'The Mighty Quinn'. Puzzled by the hesitant delivery, the freshly-pressed white suit, and by Dylan's twangy *Nashville Skyline* voice (or perhaps 'syrupy', both words are favoured by critics – listen to the Isle of Wight tracks on the *Self Portrait* album and decide), the tired, end-of-festival crowd gave the set a lukewarm reception. One year later, Jimi Hendrix was also unable to live up to the expectations of the Isle of Wight crowd at his final major performance.

'There's always those butterflies at a certain point, but then there's the realization that the songs I'm singing mean as much to the people as me, so it's just up to me to perform the best I can.'

Bob Dylan, Montreal, 1974 – at the start of a different live comeback

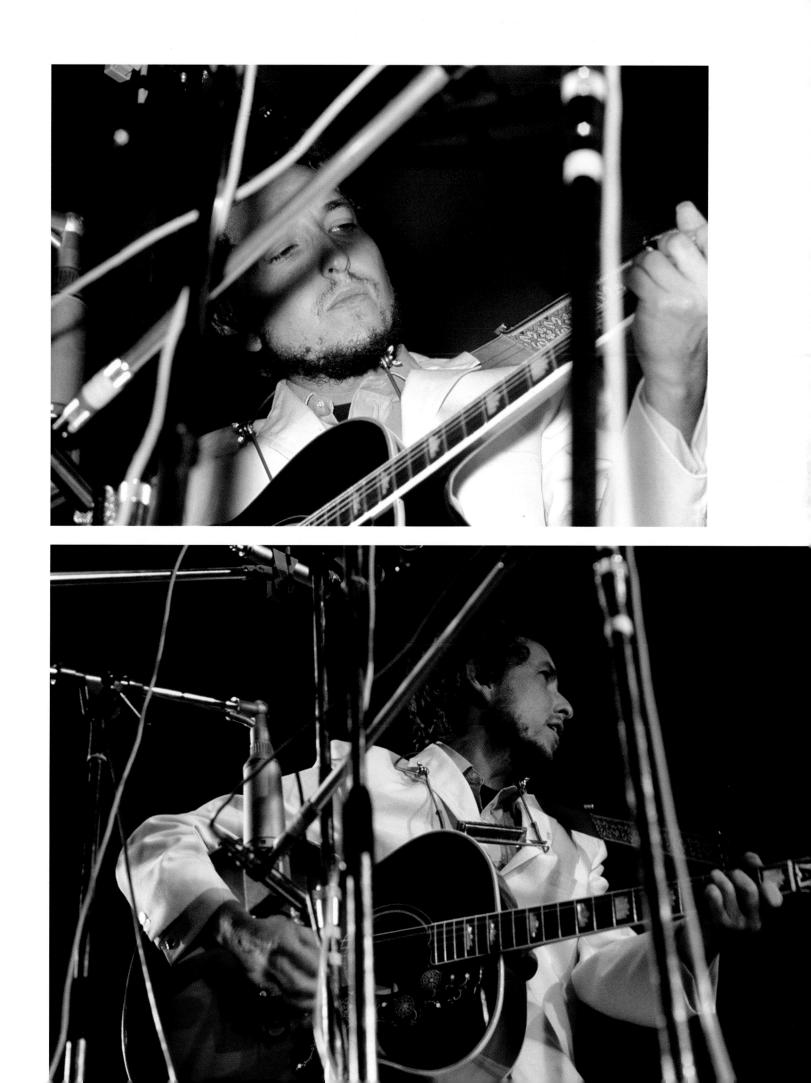

B96-4

KODAK TRI-X PAN FILM KODAK SAFETY FILM

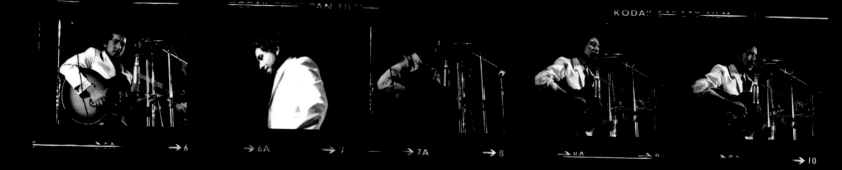

1 August 1971, Madison Square Garden, New York.
Performing at the Concert for Bangladesh, organised by George Harrison
and Ravi Shankar to raise money for refugees made homeless during the
war for Bangladesh's independence. Other stars who performed that day
included Eric Clapton, Billy Preston, Leon Russell and Ringo Starr. For
Dylan-watchers, the concert was of great significance as a rare, post-
1966, pre-1974 live performance. A visibly nervous Dylan appeared to
have abandoned his 'country' persona, and seemed ready to re-engage
with an updated take on his protest song legacy. A denim jacket, the
return of the nasal, Woody Guthrie voice and phrasing, and a set that
included 'A Hard Rain's A-Gonna Fall' and 'Blowin' in the Wind' had fans
and journalists alike in raptures. They thought they'd got the old Dylan
back. His next major move, however, was to sign up to perform in *Pat
Garrett and Billy the Kid*.

This spread and following pages:
On stage during the January to February 1974 comeback tour with The Band. Although the tour was well-received by the press, Dylan later confided in interviews that he found it to be a gruelling, unrewarding winter journey across the American heartland. There was a forthcoming album to promote, *Planet Waves* (his first complete album of new songs since 1970's *New Morning*, apart from the *Pat Garrett & Billy the Kid* soundtrack, and also the only complete studio album ever recorded with The Band) but perhaps the whole enterprise was too much a trip down memory lane for Dylan to fully enjoy it. As the tour went on, new compositions were dropped in favour of more familiar songs from the sixties. 'It's Alright Ma (I'm Only Bleeding)', with its memorable line about the President of the United States having to stand naked, drew spontaneous applause from audiences, as the Watergate saga moved nearer to its climax of Richard Nixon's resignation from office in August 1974.

Captured in profile with Robbie Robertson

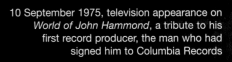

1 December 1975. The end-of-tour party for Dylan at the conclusion of the first Rolling Thunder Review. Ronnie Hawkins is wearing the hat, with his arm around Ronee Blakley. The Rolling Thunder Review brought Dylan back into a working relationship with Joan Baez, Allen Ginsberg, Bobby Neuwirth and others. The 1974 release of *Blood on the Tracks*, Dylan's seventies masterpiece, seemed to free Dylan from the burden of his achievements in the previous decade. Suddenly, comparisons with the past didn't matter. To underline this point, Dylan finally released the official version of 1967's *Basement Tapes* in the spring of 1975. The Dylan of the mid seventies seemed once again to be a vital part of the wider music scene, winning over new admirers and even pleasing his established fans. This unusual state of affairs would be temporary.

November 1976, *The Last Waltz*.
This was The Band's farewell performance, forever captured on film by
Martin Scorsese. Left to right: Joni Mitchell, Neil Young, Rick Danko,
Van Morrison, Dylan, Robbie Robertson, Ronnie Hawkins and Levon Helm
during the concluding ensemble performance of 'I Shall Be Released'.

The Last Waltz. With Robbie Robertson and Rick Danko.

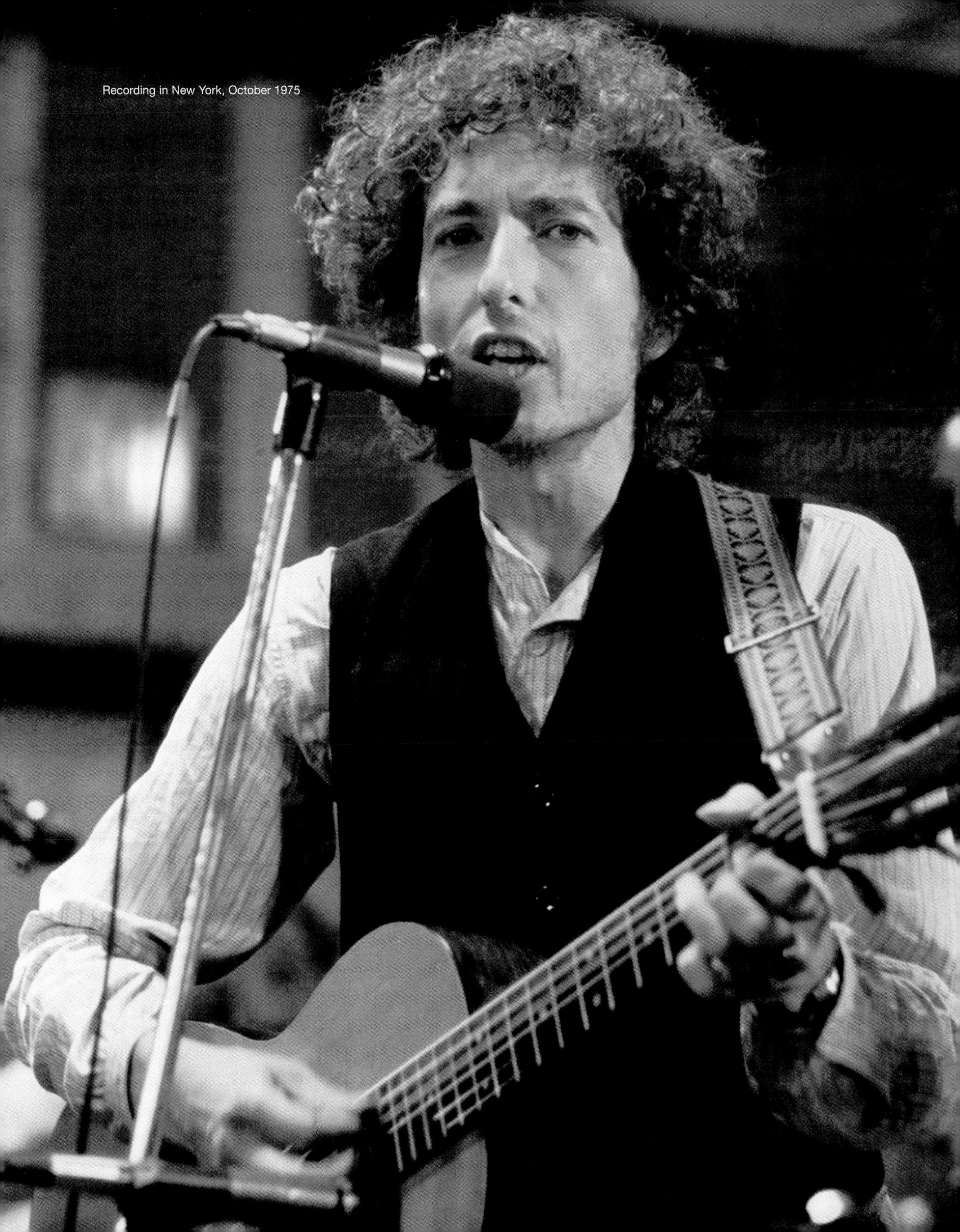
Recording in New York, October 1975

Tokyo, 1978.
A return to something resembling
the white-suited Dylan of 1969 vintage.

Earl's Court, London, June 1978.
Dylan played six sell-out dates
in the 17,000 seat arena.

The Blackbushe Picnic, 15 July 1978.

Still touring to promote his new album *Street Legal* (and, as some said at the time, to pay the cost of his divorce) Dylan headed a line-up that also included Joan Armatrading, Eric Clapton and Graham Parker. 'It's Alright Ma (I'm Only Bleeding)' once again became a highlight of the set, with Dylan's band getting their teeth into a song that is pure rock, despite having been recorded for *Bringing It All Back Home* with just Dylan accompanying himself on guitar and harmonica. The line about the President of the United States standing naked was still drawing spontaneous applause, even though Jimmy Carter was now firmly established in the White House. The Blackbushe performance was regarded as the highlight of the UK leg of Dylan's 1978 world tour. For those who could get close enough to the front to observe details, Dylan was in his impish persona – black leather jacket, top hat (!) and dark eye-liner. Alan Pasqua is on keyboards and Billy Cross on guitar. Bobbye Hall, Steve Douglas and Jerry Scheff can be seen on the extreme right.

Blackbushe, with Billy Cross and Eric Clapton

Blackbushe, July 1978

Opposite: Paris, 1981.
Dylan's 1981 set, still strongly favouring his Born Again material, went
over better on the European leg of the tour than in the USA.

Paris, 1981

Previous page:
23 June 1981, Stade de Colombes, Paris.
Steve Ripley on guitar, Jim Keltner on drums, Tim Drummond on bass.

Opposite: In concert, 1978

This spread and following pages:
The Texas Lone Star Cafe, New York, 16 February 1983. Dylan spends
time jamming with trusted former associates Rick Danko and Levon Helm.

Parc des Sceaux, Paris, 1 July 1984, with Carlos Santana on the 1984
Dylan/Santana European tour. On the left is Hughes Aufray, the French
musician who championed Dylan's songs in France.

Opposite: Slane Castle, Dublin, July 1984

With Tom Petty, 1987

Live Aid, 1985 – on stage with Ron Wood and Keith Richards

Farm Aid, 1985

On stage with the Grateful Dead, July 1987

Opposite: 1991, Hammersmith Odeon, London

Spain 1991

Phoenix Festival, Oxfordshire, England, 1995

Behind the keyboards, Sunfest, Palm Beach, Florida, May 2003.
George Recile on drums, Tony Garnier on bass.

Still behind the keyboards, Worms, Germany, June 2004

Austin, Texas, September 2007. Donny Herron on keyboards.

Opposite: New Orleans Jazzfest, April 2006

With Johnny Hallyday,
Paris 1966

Three
STILL ON THAT ROAD

'I never want anything that isn't what I've got right in front of me at any given moment.'

Bob Dylan, 2002

One of the most startling and appealing finds in the Rex Archives, when this book was being researched, were the photographs of Dylan with French rock 'n' roll star Johnny Hallyday, taken in Paris in 1966.

Who is this guy who looks exactly like Bob Dylan?

Whatever happened to the scowling, super-sensitive, doesn't-suffer-fools-gladly, anguished-conscience-of-a-generation, journalist-eating, hidden-behind-dark-sunglasses (And Other Forms Of Psychic Explosion), Garboesque High Priest of the electric folk-rock revolution?

And this Dylan impersonator seems to be having the most memorable ever, two-stars-get-together-to-hang-out, fantastic night out on the town with Hallyday, dismissed by many in the Anglophone world as a phoney Gallic Elvis Presley. What the hell is going on here?

In fact, the two singers might have had quite a lot to talk about at this particular time. Hallyday had married Sylvie Vartan in 1965. He was to become a father in August 1966, and may not have relished the responsibility. The birth of Hallyday's son ushered in a period of heavy drink and drug use for the singer, culminating in a series of suicide attempts. Dylan, likewise, had recently married (on 22 November 1965, to Sara Lownds), and had also recently become a father for the first time (his son Jesse had been born on 6 January 1966). Dylan had clearly felt, at least to begin with, that the status of a married man was not appropriate for his public image, and had kept the marriage to Sara a secret (John Lennon, of course, had been advised to do the same thing). But the news of Dylan's marriage had leaked out anyway – one more pressure, at a time when Dylan seemed to be on

permanent public show trial for having abandoned acoustic performance and the cause of protest music.

Dylan's Paris performances in May 1966 were deliberately confrontational in a way that the rest of the 1965-1966 tours had not been. The mere presence of a rock band had been enough to upset audiences in the USA and Britain, with the resultant heckling and occasional counterblasts from the stage by Dylan. But in Paris, Dylan seemed to go out of his way to antagonize his French audience, playing in front of a giant American flag (the Vietnam War was approaching its height), and making a number of remarks that implied he had limited faith in the ability of the Parisian crowd to appreciate his performance.

Leap forward a dozen years, and Dylan is back in Paris to perform. A lot has happened in the meantime – both to Dylan and the world. But the Parisian media had not forgiven Dylan. When tickets failed to sell out for Pavillon de Paris show, the Paris picture agency SIPA commented in its picture captions that 'while in America and Britain Mr Dylan is more than a myth, more than a legend, in France it seems he is just another name...'.

After his 1987 epiphany concerning a new approach to live performing (described in detail by Dylan in *Chronicles*), Dylan returned to the road on what others have called the 'Never Ending Tour'. Dylan himself dislikes this phrase. 'It annoys me when I hear people talking about The Never Ending Tour. Obviously, everything must finish. That which ties everyone together and which makes everyone equal is our mortality' (quoted from Dylan's 2002 European tour programme). One strange thing, however, is that Dylan's

Dezo Hoffmann's 1965 portrait

almost ceaseless touring over the last two decades has not delivered Dylan the performer into the role of worn-out familiar, the clichéd scenario of the passé rock star out on the road struggling to relive past glories. A Dylan concert, whatever the size of the audience, is still An Event. Dylan's public have not managed to wear out the mystique through over-exposure. In fact, the mystique seems a little stronger than it was twenty years ago, at the close of the Dylan-unfriendly eighties. Touring and playing his music to live audiences has become the central aspect of Dylan's art. New albums have become an exciting diversion along this trail.

Trying out a Fender bass, 1965

1965: a clear shot

Paris, 23 May 1966.
Press conference, with the 'Finian' puppet:
'It's a religious symbol.'

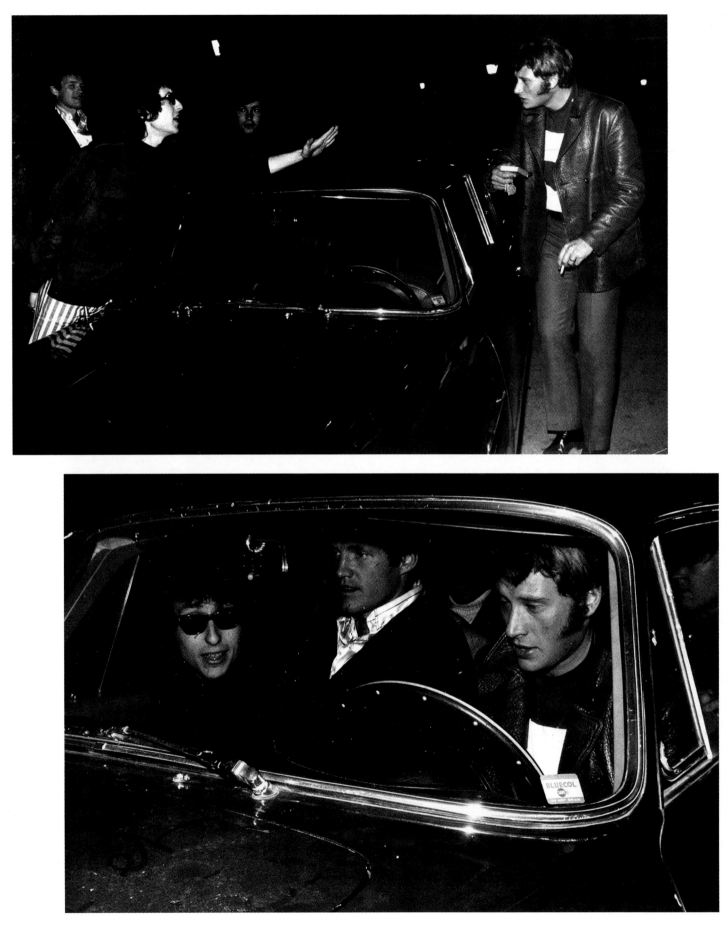

With Johnny Hallyday, Paris, 1966. Possibly taken on Dylan's 25th birthday.

Paris, World Tour, 1966. Rick Danko is on the extreme right.

Entering the Hotel George V, Paris

A few moments later. Robbie Robertson can be seen on the extreme left.

Up on the roof

Press conference, 1966

Press conference, 1966

Mayfair Hotel, London, 3 May 1966

Isle of Wight Concert poster, 1969

With Ronnie Hawkins at the Nickleodeon club bar,
Toronto, early hours of 10 January 1974.
On Dylan's left is childhood friend Lou Kemp.

Overleaf: Earl's Court, June 1978

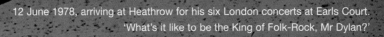

12 June 1978, arriving at Heathrow for his six London concerts at Earls Court.
'What's it like to be the King of Folk-Rock, Mr Dylan?'

Press conference, 29 May 1984, Villa Cortine Palace Hotel,
Lake Guarda, Italy. Promoter Bill Graham can be seen on the extreme left.

'Tom was at the top of his game
and I was at the bottom of mine.'

Bob Dylan, *Chronicles*, p.148

17 August 1986, outside London's National Film Theatre, where a press conference was held to publicize *Hearts of Fire*, just before principal photography commenced

Hyde Park concert, London, 1996

1965 portrait by Harry Goodwin

Four
MYSTERY TRAMP

'I would need some kind of new template, some philosophical identity that wouldn't burn out.'

Bob Dylan, *Chronicles: Volume One*, p.73

And then there are the portraiture assignments, the images of Dylan when photographer and subject are (in theory at least) working together to achieve a common goal. As well as the (relatively rare) occasions where Dylan has been captured to good effect in paparazzi shots.

In the early stages of Dylan's recording career, some of the most widely seen images of the singer were the photographs used on the album covers. Twelve-inch vinyl may not have the indelible sound quality of digital recording (a debatable point), but the size of the albums did give greater scope for inventive graphic design and imagery depicting the artist being marketed. Dylan's first album cover tells a simple story – the singer with his guitar, dressed in his folksinger's cap and suede jacket. The second album cover, *The Freewheelin'*, begins to put the singer in some kind of context, with Dylan walking down a snow-covered New York street, arm in arm with girlfriend Suze Rotolo. The third album, *The Times They Are A-Changin'*, is the first to feature a monochrome image of a solo Dylan, looking far more serious and intense than on the previous album, as befitting the unrelenting seriousness of the album's content. 1964's *Another Side of Bob Dylan* features songs that foreshadow the electric Dylan albums of the following year. The cover image, again in black and white, is of a more hip, more fashion-conscious singer, in frayed denims and pea jacket.

Things really start to get interesting on the front cover of *Bringing It All Back Home*, one of the album cover designs which arguably defined a change in the zeitgeist, alongside The Beatles' *Rubber Soul* and The Byrds' *Mr Tambourine Man*. As photographed by Daniel Kramer, Dylan, dressed as an urban pop star in an Edwardian jacket, high-buttoned collar and mauve cuff links, sits fondling a grey kitten on a multi-coloured divan or chaise-longue. Dylan languidly flicks through Dell's 1964 reissue of Hollywood gossip columnist's Louella Parsons' biography of blonde bombshell Jean Harlow. Not very 'folk' reading material. Resting on the bedside table is the 1 January 1965 issue of *Time* magazine, a journal subsequently to be the subject of Dylan's asseverations to *Time* stringer Horace Judson in *Don't Look Back*. The cover features the newly-inaugurated President Lyndon Johnson. In front of the magazine are placed an alarm clock, a radio and a mouth organ. ('...radio and records, that's where people hang out' said Dylan in August 1965.) The table on which all these items are resting is partly constructed from a Fallout Shelter sign. Lounging in the background, in a killer scarlet trouser suit, is the glamorous Sally Grossman, wife of Dylan's manager Albert Grossman. She has one arm extended, the other holds a smouldering cigarette. Every aspect of the scene and the two subjects' body language is a silent disavowal of the world of Folk and Protest singing.

The objects placed on the divan, however, are artfully selected to provide a bridge from Dylan's previous career to the new departures awaiting on the so-carefully-packaged vinyl within. In the background, behind Sally Grossman's arm, is a copy of Dylan's previous album, *Another Side of Bob Dylan*. The placing of this record, so far into the background, may imply a certain distancing from the kind of music contained therein. In the foreground, next to Dylan,

121

are an intriguingly eclectic heap of albums, including records by The Impressions, Robert Johnson, Eric Von Schmidt and Lotte Lenya – all of whom Dylan has written about as influences on his career. Behind Dylan and Sally Grossman, on the ornate, tous-les-louis mantelpiece, are further objects including paintings supposedly by Dylan himself, and an unidentified, apparently eighteenth-century portrait. On the back of the album, amongst some black and white reportage shots, we are able to pick out Joan Baez and Allen Ginsberg.

Seldom has an album cover more successfully conveyed the essence of the content enclosed, particularly the essence of Dylan's 1965 change in musical and lyric expression. Subsequent Dylan album covers never needed to work quite so hard, never needed to put across quite so much new information. *Highway 61 Revisited* shows an even more rock Dylan, wearing the previously-noted amazing blue-and-purple shirt and the much-analysed Triumph motorbike t-shirt (Dylan was riding a Triumph at the time of his July 1966 accident). *Blonde on Blonde* splashes a suede-jacketed Dylan across its double-album gatefold, but opens up to reveal a collection of enigmatic and uncaptioned stills of Dylan and friends, including Sara, and what appears to be the back of Bobby Neuwirth's head. *John Wesley Harding*, along with Dylan's characteristically enigmatic, James Thurber-style sleeve notes, features a photograph on the front of the singer accompanied by Laxman Das and Purna Das of the Bengali Bauls – itinerant musicians from India

who were invited to stay in Woodstock by Albert Grossman.

Less obviously, it has been noticed over the years that the album cover carries a secret, hidden message. Turn it upside down (you will ideally need a copy of the 12-inch vinyl album for this exercise). Stare hard at the top of the tree trunk, at the point where it is cropped by the edge of the photograph. Lurking in what seem initially to be folds of the thick bark are tiny faces, some of which have a resemblance to the faces of The Beatles, *Sgt. Pepper* vintage.

Compared to this kind of concealed communication (equivalent to the backwards phrase 'if Mars invades us' that some critics claim is deliberately included in the song 'If Dogs Run Free'), the later album covers are clear and straightforward in their impact. Dylan himself has commented on the photograph of his youthful self with Victoria Spivey, seen on the back cover of *New Morning* 'Maybe I was even making this record because I had the cover in mind and needed something to go into the sleeve' he writes in *Chronicles: Volume One*, p.139.

That's the paradox of the Mystery Tramp. The heart of his myth-making genius. Just as he seems happy to play it straight with you, to drop all pretence of hidden meaning, he lays down a remark so outrageous (if taken seriously), that every crank critic and conspiracy theorist gets to have a field day.

The images in this chapter show various facets of the off-duty Dylan, as enigmatic a performer offstage as on.

Opposite: 1965 portrait by Harry Goodwin

1965 portrait

124

The colossal shirt

The colossal shirt again

...and again.

Don't Look Back poster

Still from *Don't Look Back*

Dinner with Sara, 1975

Renaldo and Clara

Altercation with a photographer, 1977

July 1978, outside the Crazy Horse Saloon in Paris,
apparently accompanied by backing singer and
sometime collaborator, Helena Springs

17 February 1978: at a press conference in Tokyo,
on arrival for his first concert tour of Japan

31 March 1986, Chasen's Restaurant in Beverly Hills, Los Angeles, on the occasion of Dylan being presented with the Founder's Award by ASCAP, the American Society of Composers, Authors and Publishers

Out of character 1984 portrait

Paris 1984. The Keith Richards impersonation picture.

As Billy Parker in *Hearts of Fire*, another alias

Opposite and following pages:
Dylan at Heathrow Airport, 10 February 1990

The airport incident...

..., and another shot

This spread:
Camden Town, London, 21 July 1993,
with Dave Stewart, on a break from shooting
the video for 'Blood in My Eyes'. Dylan signed
autographs for passers-by, some of whom
were to appear in the finished video.

a-changing."

BOB DYLAN

BOB DYLAN

"It's not me, it's the songs. I'm just the postman. I deliver the songs." Robert Zimmerman, aka Bob Dylan, did more than just deliver the songs. An enigmatic and often aloof artist and performer, Dylan was the most influential American pop musician in the Sixties. Dylan's first classic song, "Blowin' in The Wind" was a huge hit for Peter, Paul & Mary 1963. Dylan's folk-rock songs - ful poetic personal commentary on events of the day - frequently challen and infuriated fans and critics, never failed to surprise them.

Biography

Lance Bass, with
Dylan's wax effigy,
Madame Tussaud's,
New York,
December 2002

Filming *Masked and Anonymous*, 2002

Five
WANTED MAN

'Most people don't like to work with other people, it's more difficult. It takes a lot.'

Bob Dylan, New York City Press Conference, July 1965

Dezo Hoffmann's portrait of Dylan in the Mayfair Hotel, May 1966, captures something of the essence of Dylan, 1965-66 version. In the background we observe D A Pennebaker, who is filming Dylan for what would become *Eat the Document* – Dylan's little-seen documentary based on his 1966 world tour. Much less frequently seen, in fact, than Pennebaker's own documentary of the 1965 tour, *Don't Look Back*.

Both *Don't Look Back* and *Eat the Document* comment (among many other things) on the process of being an observer and the process of being observed. The experience of being a star. The sense that stars are unreal people, that even when being themselves, they are acting a part for the entertainment or otherwise of the public. Dylan, Pennebaker's assistant Howard Alk and the Band's guitarist Robbie Robertson, spent a painstaking time during the latter part of 1966 assembling Pennebaker's raw footage into the montage of *Eat the Document*. Dylan himself was quite clear that the finished movie was not intended to be a documentary.

'What we were trying to do was to make a logical story out of this newsreel-type footage... to make a story which consisted of stars and starlets who were taking the roles of other people, just like a normal movie would do.'

[*Dylan: Behind the Shades*, Clinton Heylin, Penguin, First Edition 1991, p.179]

A *normal* movie – not a documentary. A documentary might be – well? Abnormal? A *normal* movie could be a movie where an actor – maybe an actor called Zimmerman – could play the part of a star called Bob Dylan. Something more like *Renaldo and Clara*? In any event, Dylan seemed not to recognise the concept of documentary (as practiced by Pennebaker in *Don't Look Back*), maybe because documentary presumes to present its edited montage as reality. Dylan was more interested in the acceptance of artifice on its own terms.

So Hoffmann's photograph is comparable to those moments when the mirrored doors of a wardrobe swing open opposite another mirror. In the words of William Empson:

'Two mirrors with Infinity to dine
Drink him below the table when they please'

['Dissatisfaction with Metaphysics', from *Complete Poems of William Empson*, Allen Lane, 2000]

A mirror, in a more literal way, seems to be the subject of the photograph on page 149. That is, most people take this uncredited image from the 1969 Isle of Wight pre-concert press conference to have been taken in a mirror. The framing of the panels behind, the odd appearance of Dylan's hair, everything about it seems to be the product of lateral inversion. Mirror vision. But it's not. It's a straight photograph, probably taken at the pre-Isle of Wight concert press conference – an opportunity which Dylan took to further disavow his pre-1966 persona. It just looks like a man staring into a mirror.

Interview with Mikal Gilmore, *Rolling Stone*, 22 December 2001, reprinted in *Dylan on Dylan*, p.428

As the 21st century unfolds, the camera captures Dylan as an old man, a survivor, A Man Out of Time. It's an identity that seems to sit comfortably with his recent output of songs, as well as with earlier songs still in his repertoire. Dylan as King Lear ('This Wheel's on Fire'), Dylan as Lazarus ('I Shall Be Released'). The Dylan of the twenty-first century. The contemporary Dylan who released a sequel to 'A Hard Rain's A-Gonna Fall' on the same day as the Twin Towers were destroyed. The Dylan who recorded 'Levee's Gonna Break' in the aftermath of Hurricane Katrina. For some reason, nobody else is doing this. Nobody else can, nobody else wants to, nobody else (young or old or middle-aged) seems equipped to have a stab at it. Better, safer, in the twenty-first century, to stay inside the reality/celebrity TV ambit, safer to be a part of the medium itself and not to attempt to name any of the terrors that haunt the world's imagination. It is, as Dylan himself has said, 'a time for great men to come forward.'

Songs that deal with the transformation of the singer's internal world are ubiquitous in Dylan's output, from his earliest recordings to his most recent. Some of his least regarded songs can be seen through this prism, as key signposts of Dylan's development. Songs such as 'Down the Highway' and 'Bob Dylan's Dream' on *The Freewheelin'*, which deal with self-transformation with most un-Dylan like nostalgia. Songs such as 'Black Crow Blues' 'Outlaw Blues', 'On the Road Again', 'It Takes a Lot to Laugh...', the exhausted, saturated, south-of-the-border 'Just Like Tom Thumb's Blues', the underrated 'Pledging My Time' and 'Absolutely Sweet Marie', just about every song on *The Basement Tapes* and *John Wesley Harding*, 'I Threw It All Away'. 'Tonight I'll Be Staying Here With You', 'All the Tired Horses', 'Sign on the Window', 'Tough Mama', every track on *Blood on the Tracks*, 'One More Cup of Coffee', 'New Pony', everything on *Slow Train Coming*, 'Jokerman', 'What Good Am I?', 'Highlands', 'Mississippi', 'Ain't Talkin''... this list hardly scratches the surface. Listen, for example, to the songs from *The Basement Tapes*, and they instantly communicate a desire for transformation from within, especially if one can stop listening for hidden meanings and accept the lyrics at face value – as songs of renunciation of a certain persona.

Certain societies have the belief that the camera lens is a stealer of souls. But the role of soul stealer in Dylan's career seems to be played by the interviewers and critics, Mr Jones and his professors. To read a transcript of a Dylan interview can sometimes be akin to watching a soul-stealer being outmanoeuvred at his work. Facing up to the man who has affected them by his songs, the interviewer grasps at something more – some answer, some interpretation, some decoding that goes beyond the work of the artist as presented. Instead, they encounter the personality of Bob Dylan, the persona created to articulate these songs. As John Cohen remarks, with great candour, in his 1968 *Sing Out* interview with Dylan: 'I can't just say to your face that you did something great, that I admire you.' The camera is tougher than this, less inflected. It doesn't permit retractions or second thoughts. It treats everyone alike, at face value. Maybe it can even record from the outside the transformation of an internal world.

This chapter gathers together photographs of Dylan with other stars and performers, from Van Morrison at Slane Castle, Dublin in 1984 to Elizabeth Taylor at a Hollywood party a decade later. Celebrities 'give off heat', as William Goldman once trenchantly observed 'and we all want to be near the fire'. Even fellow celebrities like to be near each other's glow. But Dylan doesn't seem to respond in that way. Look at these pictures and judge for yourself. They look more like a set of pictures of Dylan with people that he happens to work with sometimes. Dylan may be a mirror for others, but he doesn't appear to use his peer group in the same way.

The final image in this chapter holds up the mirror from the opposite side of the gender divide: Cate Blanchett as a wonderfully convincing mid-sixties Dylan in the 2007 movie *I'm Not There*. Directed by Todd Haynes, the film delivers an intelligent and original dissection of Dylan's career. Six actors play different aspects of Dylan's multi-faceted persona: Marcus Carl Franklin the young hobo guitarist, Christian Bale the protest singer, Ben Whishaw the poet, Cate Blanchett the *Blonde on Blonde* electric rocker, the late Heath Ledger the reclusive star and family man, and Richard Gere a kind of surreal, wandering Billy the Kid who has stepped out of the Peckinpah movie into a remote part of the backwoods, inhabited by refugees from the *Basement Tapes* songs and deranged members of a Wild West Travelling Medicine Show. All the performances are strong, with Blanchett's, Ledger's and Franklin's being outstanding. The movie avoids obvious rhetoric about fame and stardom, focusing its energy instead on the rich texture of its subject matter, which is wisely allowed to speak for itself. From time to time, the role of Bob Dylan may be up for grabs by other performers.

This spread and following pages:
With Joan Baez, Victoria Embankment in London, 28 April 1965.
The tour was filmed for the documentary *Don't Look Back*, which traces
Dylan's changing relationship with his fans, as well as with Baez.

'Me and Joan?... She brought me up...
I rode on her, but I don't think I owe her
anything... I feel bad for her because she
has nobody to turn to that's going to be
straight with her....'

Interview with Robert Shelton, from *No Direction Home*,
March 1966, reprinted in *Dylan on Dylan*, p.88

Opposite top: With Van Morrison, Slane Castle, Dublin, 8 July 1984
Opposite below: With Ronnie Wood, 1985

With Bruce Springsteen, 28/29 January 1985,
reocrding 'We are the World' at A&M Studios in Los Angeles

Opposite: Publicity shoot for *Hearts of Fire*, 1986

With Fiona Flanagan and Rupert Everett, 17 August 1986: a press
conference at London's National Film Theatre to publicize *Hearts of Fire*

Opposite top: 'We are the World', with Bette Midler
Opposite below: With Bruce Springsteen and Mick Jagger,
Rock Hall of Fame Awards, New York 1988

Overleaf: Bob Dylan Tribute Concert, Madison Square Garden,
New York, 1992 – Ronnie Wood, Johnny Cash, George Harrison,
Roger McGuinn, June Carter and Dylan

With Don Johnson at the Clinton Inauguration, January 1993

With Elizabeth Taylor at Chasen's Restaurant in Los Angeles, on the occasion of Dylan's receipt of the Founder's award from ASCAP, the American Society of Composers, Authors and Publishers

With
Cheech Marin,
on *Masked and
Anonymous*

With
Angela Bassett,
on *Masked and
Anonymous*

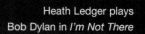
Heath Ledger plays
Bob Dylan in *I'm Not There*

Cate Blanchett plays
Bob Dylan in *I'm Not There*

Amnesty International concert,
Los Angeles, 1986

AFTERWORD

If you are already familiar with Dylan's work, this book of photographs may have – with luck – intrigued or amused you with some previously unseen images of the Glass Onion, the Buddha in European Dress. You will certainly not need to be led back to Dylan's music, his songs, and other writings. But if – by some remarkable chance – this volume is your first encounter with Dylan and his work, then your appetite may have been whetted for the real thing. But where to start? There are so many albums (over 50!), so many interpretive writings, so many documentaries, and – now – a significant quantity of Dylan's own words in print.

A serious roadmap for the beginner would be *The Rough Guide to Bob Dylan*. It's a humbling thought that such a volume exists, and needs to exist. But before embarking on that book, and the many others that it will lead to, here is a very brief and (I hope) objective overview of Dylan's work and his career.

Albums

Dylan's reputation rests on the albums he recorded in the sixties. Some of the later work may offer a challenge to these in terms of quality, but without the sixties albums there would be no Dylan as we currently perceive him. The sixties Dylan albums fall into three phases. First, the acoustic albums *Bob Dylan*, *The Freewheelin'*, *The Times They Are A-Changin'* and *Another Side of Bob Dylan*. *Bob Dylan* is Dylan's first album. It's mainly an album of covers, representing an aspect of the singer's work when he first

arrived in New York. Fascinating, but perhaps not the ideal place to begin, unless chronological development rules your world. *The Freewheelin'* is another story, an essential album and one of Dylan's personal favourites, containing several of his most famous early songs: 'Blowin' in the Wind', 'Masters of War', 'A Hard Rain's A-Gonna Fall'. *The Times They Are A-Changin'* contains more 'finger pointing' songs, including the eponymous title track and 'With God On Our Side'. Some critics have found this album to be a little unrelenting and heavy-handed when compared to *The Freewheelin'*. *Another Side of Bob Dylan* is just that – an album devoid of protest material, which foreshadows many of the lyrical themes and musical styles of the next phase of the singer's development. 'Chimes of Freedom' and 'To Ramona' are perhaps the best-known songs from this album.

As everyone knows, Dylan controversially 'went electric' in 1965 – first in the studio, then at the Newport Folk Festival. *Bringing It All Back Home*, the first album to be built around Dylan and a backing band, only uses the band on its first side, for songs such as 'Subterranean Homesick Blues' and 'Maggie's Farm'. Side two features visionary songs with acoustic arrangements, including 'Mr Tambourine Man' and 'It's Alright Ma (I'm Only Bleeding)'. Over the years, Dylan has kept more songs from this album in his touring set lists than from any other. *Bringing It All Back Home* was followed rapidly by *Highway 61 Revisited* and *Blonde on Blonde* – both also essential Dylan albums. 'Like a Rolling Stone' – perhaps Dylan's best-known rock song – opens *Highway 61 Revisited*, and the level of inspiration never flags from that incandescent opening right through to the final track 'Desolation Row'. *Blonde on Blonde* was the first album Dylan recorded in Nashville. Despite this relocation, the record sounds like a logical progression from *Highway 61 Revisited*. The lyrics, perhaps even darker and more cynical than on the previous album, are set against music that employs wit, irony and pastiche as well as the out-and-out power of a backing band that includes Robbie Robertson and Al Kooper. The sustained mood – as in both the previous two albums – makes the whole greater than the sum of its parts. Comparatively throwaway songs such as 'Leopard-Skin Pillbox Hat' draw depth from their association with, say, 'Visions of Johanna', while the poker-face parodies such as 'Fourth Time Around' act like helium in the mix with the more introspective pieces such as 'I Want You' and the epic 'Sad Eyed Lady of the Lowlands'. Some of Dylan's best-loved songs from the 1965-66 period, such as 'Positively 4th Street' and 'Can You Please Crawl Out Your Window' do not appear on any of the original studio albums, and have to be sought out elsewhere.

Dylan's next phase of recording came in the wake of his motorcycle accident in July 1966. At first content to rest, recuperate and spend time with his young family in upstate New York, Dylan began rehearsing and recording with The Band in the basement of Big Pink, The Band's Woodstock residence. Traditional, unpolished, ornery, direct from America's cracker barrel, the results – *The Basement Tapes* – were not officially released until 1975. Curiously undervalued by Dylan, who regarded the songs as simply demos for other artists and a fulfilment of contractual commitments, the critical reputation of *The Basement Tapes* has grown steadily over the years, unsurprising for a collection that includes such Dylan classics as 'Tears of Rage', 'Nothing Was Delivered' and 'This Wheel's on Fire', and which defines what amounts to a new hybrid between rock and roll, blues, country and folk music. *The Basement Tapes* also bridge the otherwise confusing stylistic gulf between *Blonde on Blonde* and Dylan's next official release, *John Wesley Harding*. Stripped down to a backing band of just drums and bass, *John Wesley Harding*, along with *The Basement Tapes*, make a compelling case that Dylan reached his absolute creative peak in 1967 – if such judgements amount to anything. 'All Along The Watchtower' epitomises the lyrical power and sense of moral and spiritual unease that underpin this recording, though the last two songs, 'Down Along the Cove' and 'I'll Be Your Baby Tonight' look forward to the mellow, relaxed mood of *Nashville Skyline* – an album deliberately designed to sound 'bridled and housebroken' according to Dylan's own account of it in *Chronicles: Volume One*.

It is not so easy to find a consistent thread of development in Dylan's albums of the seventies. 1970's *Self Portrait*, the double album of cover versions, has few enthusiasts. The follow-up *New Morning*, also from 1970, contains a handful of strong, interesting songs (such as 'Went to See the Gypsy'), but may have been made to seem better than it was by being released so soon after the unloved *Self Portrait*. *Pat Garrett & Billy The Kid* is a soundtrack album, the standout song being the hit single 'Knockin' on Heaven's Door'. *Planet Waves* was Dylan's first and only official studio album with The Band. Much admired on its appearance in 1974, at the end of a long Dylan drought, its reputation has declined over the years, and might be overdue for a reappraisal. 'Tough Mama', Dylan's song addressed to his recalcitrant muse, is an intriguing, gutsy song unjustly ignored by both Dylan and the critics alike. *Planet Waves* was soon overshadowed by Dylan's seventies masterpiece *Blood on the Tracks*. Containing such songs as 'Tangled Up In Blue' and 'Idiot Wind', it is regarded by many as the equal of Dylan's mid-sixties work, and is a recording of immense significance as it freed Dylan the songwriter from living in the shadow of his earlier, anthemic compositions. *Desire*, an album dominated instrumentally by Scarlet Rivera's violin, marks a return to social engagement ('Hurricane', 'Joey'), as well as including several deeply personal songs ('Sara'), and has the unique additional dimension of sleeve notes by the poet Allen Ginsberg. 1978's *Street Legal* is a lightweight album by comparison, but 1979's *Slow Train Coming* unveiled Dylan's conversion to Born Again Christianity. Whatever the impact of Dylan the Hellfire Preacher's lyrics, the music and the overall sound of *Slow Train Coming* are very powerful.

There is something incompatible between the words 'Bob Dylan' and 'the 1980s'. In the decade of Reagan, Thatcher, yuppies, red braces, *Dallas*, *Dynasty* and Hugo Boss suits, there seemed to be no natural place for Dylan's music. Dylan was more prolific on record during the eighties than the seventies, but his releases during the decade are of variable quality. 1980 and 1981 saw the completion of the 'Born Again' trilogy with *Saved* and *Shot of Love*. 1984's *Infidels* is one of the decade's most interesting Dylan releases, built around the Sly Dunbar/Robbie Shakespeare rhythm section, and featuring songs as varied as 'Jokerman', 'Man of Peace' and 'Don't Fall Apart on Me Tonight'.

Empire Burlesque followed in 1985, 'Tight Connection to My Heart' being the track most favourably received by the critics and welcomed into Dylan's live set. *Knocked Out Loaded* and *Down in the Groove*, a covers album, were not well received, but Dylan ended the eighties with his best album of the decade, *Oh Mercy*. The circumstances surrounding the making of this album are related in Dylan's

Filming *Hearts of Fire* at Colston Hall,
Bristol, September 1986

Filming *Masked and Anonymous*
on location in Los Angeles, July 2002

Chronicles: Volume One, and a track listing including 'Ring Them Bells', 'Man in the Long Black Coat', 'What Good Am I?' , 'Disease of Conceit' and 'Shooting Star' made it clear that Dylan had overcome his case of writer's block and was very much back on form.

Since the 1980s, Dylan's activity on stage has been relentless, but his production of new recordings has been less so. Under the Red Sky (1990) was taken as a disappointing follow-up to Oh Mercy. Good as I Been to You and World Gone Wrong feature cover versions. Dylan's next album of original songs was Time Out of Mind, his last album of new songs of the twentieth century. 'Highlands' is an epic track, a song that opens up the theme of ageing, a major preoccupation of Dylan's later work. 'Love Sick' became associated with Dylan's controversial appearance in a Victoria's Secret lingerie advert. There was something reassuring about the way in which, as the century that gave us Dylan drew to its close, critics still felt it necessary to scrutinize Dylan's most casual and impulsive activities for signs that he was 'selling out' his vision.

Dylan has released two albums of new material to date in the twenty-first century. Love and Theft – released on 11 September 2001 – is a multi-faceted work. The sense of dark brooding over the direction of world events that is manifest in songs such as 'Tweedle Dee & Tweedle Dum' and 'High Water' (a kind of sequel to 'A Hard Rain's A-Gonna Fall') made this Dylan's most zeitgeist-grabbing recording since the late sixties. In a quite different mood, 'Moonlight' is an old man's love song, and utterly charming in that vein. 'Times Have Changed', the Oscar-winning song from the film Wonder Boys, does not appear on any original Dylan album, and must be sought out separately. Like 'High Water', 'Times Have Changed' very clearly references an earlier song, 'The Times They Are A-Changin''. 2006's Modern Times became Dylan's first album to top the American charts since Desire. Even more than Love and Theft, this feels like the work of a man aware of his mortality. Songs such as 'The Levee's Gonna Break' and 'Ain't Talkin'' have a cumulative expressive power that no one else but Dylan could pull off in quite the same way.

Movies

The movies and TV specials are the most immediate way to be fully immersed into the wider Dylan experience. Dylan has appeared in some outstanding movies, and also some lesser productions. Those listed below might be the best places to start.

Don't Look Back, directed by D.A. Pennebaker, 1967
Eat the Document, directed by Bob Dylan, 1972
Pat Garrett and Billy the Kid, directed by Sam Peckinpah, 1973
The Last Waltz, directed by Martin Scorsese, 1976
Hard Rain, directed by Howard Alk, 1976
Renaldo and Clara, directed by Bob Dylan, 1978
Masked and Anonymous, directed by Larry Charles, 2003
No Direction Home: Bob Dylan, directed by Martin Scorsese, 2005

Books by Bob Dylan

Tarantula, First Edition, MacGibbon & Kee, 1971
Writings & Drawings, First Edition, Jonathan Cape, 1972
Chronicles: Volume One, Simon & Shuster, 2004
Dylan on Dylan, Edited by Jonathan Cott, Penguin, 2007

Other Books

Select list of books about Bob Dylan and other books cited in the text.

Bob Dylan, Anthony Scaduto, First Edition, Grosset & Dunlap, 1971
Bob Dylan: Behind the Shades, Clinton Heylin, First Edition, Penguin, 1991
Bob Dylan: In His Own Words, Compiled by Miles (aka Barry Miles), First Edition, Omnibus, 1978
Bob Dylan: Performing Artist Volume 1 1960-1973: The Early Years, Paul Williams, Omnibus, 1994
Bob Dylan: Performing Artist Volume 2 1974-1986: The Middle Years, Paul Williams, Omnibus, 1994
Bob Dylan: Performing Artist Volume 3: Mind Out Of Time 1986 And Beyond, Paul Williams, Omnibus, 2004
Do You, Mr Jones?, Neil Corcoran, Pimlico, 2003
If They Move... Kill 'Em: The Life and Times of Sam Peckinpah, David Weddle, Grove Press, 1994
Million Dollar Bash: Bob Dylan, The Band and The Basement Tapes, Sid Griffin, Jawbone Press, 2007
Moondust, Andrew Smith, Bloomsbury, 2006
Positively 4th Street: The Lives and Times of Joan Baez, Bob Dylan, Mimi Baez Farina and Richard Farina, David Hajdu, North Point Press, 2002
The Rough Guide to Bob Dylan, Nigel Williamson, Rough Guide, 2006
Song and Dance Man III: The Art of Bob Dylan, Michael Gray, Continuum, 2000

PICTURE CREDITS

All references are by page numbers.

INDEX

K SAF.ETY FILM

KODAK SAF.ETY FILM

KODAK TRI-X PAN FILM

KODAK TRI-X PAN FILM

KODAK TRI-X PAN FILM